LORETTA HAWKINS

THE BRIGHTNESS OF FIRE

POEMS FROM
ANOTHER TIME

Loretta A. Hawkins

LORETTA HAWKINS

Requests for permission to make copies of any part of this work should be email to:

hawkinsloretta@gmail.com

firekeeperartistry@gmail.com

ISBN-13: 978-0-692-13060-5

First Edition

LORETTA HAWKINS

THE BRIGHTNESS OF FIRE

PUBLISHED BY

FIREKEEPER ARTISTRY

CHICAGO, ILLINOIS

DEDICATION

The Brightness of Fire: Poems From Another Time is dedicated to my three children, Robin, Dionne and Sherri. I dedicate these poems, written so long ago, to them because they were the nourishing spirits that surrounded me when these poems were conceived, manifested and written. They, who shared a dwelling with me at that time in their lives, filled mine with joy, happiness, anxiety, laughter, and all of the emotions evoked in rearing children. They were my constant, my always there, my place called home. They were, and are, my children. I am extraordinarily proud of them for the women they have become: kind, hardworking, honest, accomplished, and loving. What more could a mother want from her children? I love them with every fiber of my being and know that they are the greatest gifts ever given to me.

The Brightness of Fire: Poems From Another Time is also dedicated to my mother, Laurine (Blink) Hines Sanders, for it is my mother who instilled in me the life values and teachings that I passed on to my children, for she was the most gentle, kindest, generous, and loving soul that I have encountered on my journey through life. My love for her is never-ending and always there. She is the personification of love, for I can never remember a time in my life that I was not consumed with the love I have for her.

The Brightness of Fire: Poems From Another Time is dedicated to the bridge that connects three generations of African-American women in America, striving to live our lives to the fullest while inspiring others simply by the manner in which we attempt to live the best life we can, harming no others, helping those we can, and loving others as much as possible. I am proud of the generations before me, and the generations after me, hoping that I, in return, can make them both as proud of me.

ACKNOWLEDGEMENTS

"Bubble Gum and Common Things" first appeared in *Major Poets*. "Statement on Child Abuse" first appeared in *Mountain View Digest*. "Dream Stuff" first appeared in *Broken Glass*. "Must We Wait" and "Afrique Unique" first appeared in *Malcolm X-Emplar* and "The Last Day" first appeared in *Tears in the Fence*, Dorcet, England. "Masquerade" first appeared in *Slick Press Poetry Magazine* and "Of Men and War" first appeared in *The Cranium*. "Afternoon in Late July" first appeared in *The Creative Woman Magazine*. "Beer Gardens Near Diamonds and Gold" was first published in *Exit 13*.

Grateful acknowledgement is made to these periodicals.

"I use to write about different things.
'Bout Emmett Till and Malcolm X, 'bout Rodney King.
'Bout unjust laws, human rights, and youthful dreams."

From "I Use to Write" by Loretta A. Hawkins

THE BRIGHTNESS OF FIRE

PREFACE
The Brightness of Fire
Poems From Another Time

The Brightness of Fire: Poems From Another Time is a collection
of poems written many years ago when I was a young woman.
They are a plaintive cry into the wind, an accusation of the
injustices and racial oppression that existed at that time, for I was a
young adult before I was legally allowed to sit on the front of a
public bus in the small southern town where I was born. Restricted
to the back of the bus, and legally obligated to give up my seat,
even there, to any white person without a seat, was but one of
hundreds of laws that were designed to establish and subsequently
ensure that I remain inferior, unequal, and disenfranchised, and in
the mind of the oppressors, less than human.

Coming of age in the sixties, I, along with millions of other Blacks
in America, was frustrated, angry, and resolved. We looked with
clear eyes at the events of the day, waiting for the movement that
would propel us out of the alternate reality where we dwelled and
into the real world. We literally suffered when we saw Emmett
Till's mutilated body, either in person in Chicago, or on the cover
of Jet Magazine. We could never forget. Every public lynching
thereafter was stamped on our psyche.

We grew furious when Muhammad Ali's Championship boxing
belt was stolen from him because he refused to, as he said, fight or
kill some colored people who had never called him nigger or done
anything to hurt him. We would not forget. We were insulted when
Rosa Parks was arrested for refusing to give up her seat in the
colored section of a public bus so that a white man could sit down.
We would not forget.

We were enraged when four white policemen who struck Rodney King fifty-six times in eighty-one seconds were found innocent of police brutality. So enraged were we that we did not remember that Dr. King had said that a riot is the language of those who have no voice. And because we were socially mute, the cities of America burned with the brightness of fire.

Our heroes became Stokely Carmichael, Malcolm X, Martin Luther King, Jr., Angela Davis. Rap Brown, Nelson Mandela, Huey Newton, The Honorable Minister Louis Farrakhan, Bobby Seales and the Black Panthers. for they were the ones we had been waiting for. The poems in this collection are of those times, those people and those injustices. These are the events, people and ideas about which poets write.

But because forgiveness is the disciplined decision to give up one's justified right for revenge, black people today, I surmise, have forgiven white America for its past sins. We have forgiven. But for the sins of today, there must be repentance before forgiveness.

Because of the Barack Obama presidency, it is easy to believe that race relations have improved in the United States since the end of slavery. The fact of the matter, however, is that regarding racial justice, conditions for African –Americans have deteriorated and have become overtly worse. In 1866, the year after slavery ended, the Black Codes were passed into law. Created to govern, restrict, control, and limit every aspect of a black person's life, the Black Codes were laws simultaneously ubiquitous and over-powering. One such law prevented blacks from carrying weapons at the risk of being arrested. Today, however, a black person carrying a gun, frequently is executed on the spot, no questions asked, with impunity. This has happened to the extent that the killing of an un-armed black person, *running away*, is now a normal phenomenon. Indeed, many offenses for which blacks were previously arrested, are now death sentences. These poems, for the most part, are a wail into the wind for justice and equality.

CONTENTS

LORETTA HAWKINS

THE BRIGHTNESS OF FIRE

THE BRIGHTNESS OF FIRE

I

...being me

Summary of World Civilization - I

First of all, they killed Jesus Christ.
Near a place called Jerusalem.
They crucified him because
he was going around making strange
And preposterous claims.

But before that, they killed Socrates.
Very civilized, of course, with hemlock;
for after all, this was the height
of Greek civilization. In Athens.
Socrates was advocating change
and saying stuff about right and wrong
that Jesus Himself would later quote.

After Jesus was Abraham Lincoln. In America.
He had the audacity to emancipate the slaves
of an entire nation. Just set them free.
They weren't even his own slaves but
he believed in abolition. And change.
He was shot in a theater.

Next was Mahatma Gandhi. In India.
He was setting folks free, too
with passive resistance, non-violence,
and civil disobedience, so he, too had
to be assassinated. He was shot three times.

John Kennedy, an American, came along.

Talking about change. Talking about
freedom and <u>disenfranchisement</u>.
And quoting Lincoln. They shot him
in the neck and in the head.

Martin Luther King, Jr. - America in Alabama.
same thing. talking about change.
about freedom. And quoting Gandhi.
When King was in jail, he wrote in a letter,
"<u>Injustice</u> anywhere is a threat to justice
everywhere." They killed him, too.
That was after he got the Nobel Prize.

This is my summary of World Civilization I.
I have named the people and where they lived.
What I learned from this summary is
if you think too much, or try to change
anything, or set people free, or quote somebody,
they will probably kill you.

I have quoted somebody but
only because it was an assignment.
Also, I have used and underlined
all of my <u>vocabulary</u> words.

Bubble Gum And Common Things

The grandiose, the mystic, cosmic
planes
are far too broad my mind to
comprehend
and when, forgetfully it drifts
towards
such mind-expanding thoughts or
after-thoughts

my mind, indeed, does travel into
space
and seemingly expand and concentrically
thin
much like a single drop of liquid dye
dropped
in a crystal liquid universe. and
frightfully
I concentrate quite fast.... on
chewing
bubble gum and common things.

masquerade

sometimes
I think that you and I
and anyone and everyone
are masquerading life
as if attendance at such a party
put ideas into our gullible maybe-minds.

.... and so we grope through our
earthly hereness, pretending
that we live.

The Book That I Write

The book that I write will have
the compassion of James, walking stoically
in pain beneath a cold gray sky

the astonishment of Celie when she discovered
the beauty of the color purple

the poetry of Janie as, in darkness,
her eyes watched God

and the clarity of Pecola's only seconds before
hers became the bluest.

It will stride along, at various paces,
like the long life of Miss Jane Pittman

It will hold its head high like the Joads, seeking
paradise in the valley of a Californian hell

It will have music, like that which sings
throughout The Pearl

And it will be as determined as an old man single-handedly
battling sharks on a lonely azure sea.

It will cry a little, softly whimpering like Sounder,
under a weather-beaten porch

It'll scream in outrage, like Kunta Kinte when he
    discovered that there *was* something greater than
    he, besides the universe

It will throw its head back and
    laugh at life's absurdities

And whisper about the horrible thing that happened
    to the Corregidoras

It will be as warm and brown
    as the nurturing good earth

And as glorious as the coming of age
    of a manchild in a promised land

It will even dare to question
    irrational realities

And mildly wonder for whom
    the bells toll

And then it will soft away, soft away
    as quietly as mice and women

And those who read it will know
    that that was the only way
    it could possibly end.

...being me

Of late i cry without abate
and seemingly there's no escape
from dreams and fears i have of you
romancing others when we're through.

and foolishly i question you
arising swift my fears anew
and you pretend that you don't know
that i'm afraid you'll someday go.

We play this game, that i will lose
for i have not the proper tools
of fortitude, security
and knowledge that you do love me.

And when i lose, i hope to be
a stronger personality
with faith that next i love a man
i play the game the best i can
by being me.

Dream Stuff

Florida broke off and floated away
Those that could, leaped ashore and
ran non-stop to California because
they were the sun-worshippers.
California quaked and
Swallowed up everyone.

Then I awoke and stared as my bed
with me in it
slowly slid into a huge crevice.

The First Time I Saw Paris

The first time I saw Paris,
and I have only seen it once,
was in my heart.

I distinctly remember
I was in French class
in high school,
wishing I were instead, in Paris.

The teacher, Miss Luicetto,
at the front board
was conjugating verbs, *en Francois.*
"Ja vais," she said. *"Tu vas."*

I closed my eyes and tried
hard, to think of everything French I knew.

French toast, french fries, french kissing...
Nothing came.
French rolls, French cuff, French dressing...
Still nothing.

"Il va," Miss Lucietto said. *"Elle va."*
French door, French braids, French bread...
"Nous allons," came from the front.

French Provincial furniture,
French leave,

French...

Then suddenly, miraculously,
for one entire second in time
I saw Paris!

My mind euphorically wandered
through it, floating, moving,
seeing. Seeing bohemians

creating ferociously on
the Left Bank, seeing the Arc de
Triomphe, The Eiffel Tower, The Louvre,
the Champs Elysees, the timeless lovers.

The bells of Notre Dame deafened me
While the waters of the Seine
stung my nostrils with
its ancient mustiness.

And I could see all of French history
in that eternal second, like a drowning
mind, passing before my eyes.

There was Guy de Maupassant talking to
Jean Francois Champollion, and over there
Jean Valjean, moments after he was sentenced
to forty years in prison,
for stealing a piece of bread.

And there, Madeline, in two straight lines
breaking hers, saying her prayers and

going to bed.
I could see the Count of Monte Cristo being
chased by the three musketeers...

And somewhere above it all,
I could see the hunchback
of Notre Dame swinging from
heavy ropes high above
azure Parisian skies.

My eyes continued upward
noting that the Parisian skies
looked very much like
the skies of Chicago.

"Vous allez," came softly from the front.
I opened my eyes and looked out the window.
It *was* the same sky.
The *exact* same sky I had just seen in Paris.

The bell rang. Miss Lucietto put her chalk
down and said, *"Ils vont."*
I closed my book, got up, and
went to biology.

Duce & The Cord Et

Teacher read a poem in class today,
called Duce and the Cord Et
It was all about some guy
fighting some war, somewhere.
I didn't understand it!

Poem started out and this guy
and his buddies was going somewhere.
They're tired, hurt, hungry, scared,
feet bleeding, no shoes. Just f---ed up!
Then the enemy drop some gas shells on them.

Now the way that works is—when the shells drop
if you don't have a gas mask on
the gas is inhaled straight to your lungs.
There, it turns to liquid and you drown,
on dry land! Neat trick!

So in this dumb poem, when the shells drop,
they all grab their gas masks, see?
All except one dude who can't get his on
fast enough. So he gets to drown.

He starts doing this weird dying dance
like he's being attacked by Aliens III's
or something. Then he dies.
While he's dying, they throw him up
on some wagon, taking him somewhere.

Then the guy tells how all this cud stuff comes
outta his mouth...Wait, I've got a copy.
Here it is, "If you could hear at every jolt, the blood
Come gargling from the froth-corrupted lungs
Bitten as the cud
Of vile, incurable sores on innocent tongues,-"

Yuck! Grossed me out! Why somebody wants to
write such a nasty poem, anyhow?
Then down at the end of the poem
they talk about the cord eating again.
I think it et some pot from a tree
or some marijuana.

I know I sure didn't understand it.
Anyway, I know one thing.
After reading that poem, I ain't
never going to go to nobody's war!

*Dulce et decorum est pro patria mori. (It is sweet and fitting to
die for one's country.) "Dulce Et Decorum Est" is the ironic title
of a poem by Wilfred Owen, bitterly denouncing war. The
quotation is from that poem.

Afternoon In Late July

The children were angry
because while they worked.
I sat reading nikki
giovanni and about how
cotton candy behaves and
it was not a rainy day.
in fact, it was sunny
and they wanted to go out to play… they said.
what they meant was
they wanted to go out
to talk to the boys…
needed to go out
to talk to the boys…
because
they were girls
and did not know
much (anything)
about boys.

So as one cleaned
the bathroom and the other
the oven,

they rolled their eyes
from time to time
in my direction…
one even ventured to say,
"that book is stupid"
I defended it,

"it's helping me," I said
the other one said meaningfully,
"I wish it could help us."

I ignored the remark
and as I turned
the page and began
to read about saving
poems

for the winter of her
dreams (how poetic)
my children continued
to yearn
for what they wanted
to do
while I did what I
had to do.

Everythang Was Real

the gov'ment got a new program, i understand
call it Nutritional Education - Phase One
they say they gonna learn us how to cook
and got the whole thang writ up in a book,

they say they gonna show us how to cook
with foods that'll make us strong - improve our looks -
they say...
well, all that's fine and good enough with me
but here's something i reckon they don't see,

my grandma say that when she was a child
her grandma told her when
she was a child
how there was not no food at all - for us
but black folks didn't put up any fuss,
when master got his bacon, ham and chops
then throwed the rest away, (it was not good)
why, black folks simply got them no-good parts
and cleaned them good, then cooked them half to death,

then into wild-fields growing by, they went
and pulled up greens that mother earth had sent
and these they cleaned and cooked them in a pot
till they was soft and dark and piping hot,

they pulled some sweet potatoes from the ground
that when they went a-looking, there they found

then with a little corn they made some bread
then sat down to the table - bowed they heads
and laid they eyes upon a scrumptious feast
that taught our folk, "the less is not the least"

that table held, Lord, chitt'lins, piping hot
and greens that almost made a body shout
and sweet potatoes, roasted in the hearth
and cornbread that was music of the earth,
and mercy, how them folks would eat they fill
and t'was no dream, naw, everythang was real
well, i say, if a folk know how to cook
when there ain't nothing there for them *to* cook
it seems to me that folk like that *can* cook
and we don't need to read that from no book,

they say they gonna learn us how to cook
and even writ the nonsense in a book
i'm waiting hard for Phase Two - to come due
i 'spect that's gonna learn us how to chew.

II

AFRICAN CHANTS

The Last Day

South Africaan government's
Minister of Race
announced that tomorrow
is the last day
individuals can apply
to have their race
changed... legally.

After tomorrow
he emphasized,
you will have to
remain
whatever race
you were assigned
last year.

Beer Gardens Near Diamonds and Gold

In the graveyard
of Dimbaza, infant
graves are dug
the day before,
to cradle babies
that will die within
the night.

By the graveyard
of Dimbaza, mothers
wail hopelessly
not understanding that
starvation of her child
has little to do with her
or the child itself,
but much with greed
and power gone-corrupt.

Near the graveyard
of Dimbaza, fathers
are conspicuous
in their absence,
dwelling far away instead
with no superfluous
appendages, while dying
lives of dire desperation
in beer gardens near mines of diamonds and gold.

My Father is Like a Tiger

After I leave school today,
I will go to bury my mother.
There will be no funeral because
the Africaan government
has sent out a decree
that relatives of those killed yesterday,
are on house arrest.

House arrest means that we cannot
gather in groups of three or more.
One cannot have a funeral with only
two people mourning.

My mother was marching yesterday
with a group of other mothers.
They were protesting the learning
of Africaan, in this school.

Africaan is spoken *only* in
South Africa. It is the language
of the white man who has stolen
our country, our customs, our land,
and now are going after our language.

My mother was marching, yesterday,
along with hundreds of other mothers,

They were singing! Singing to God!
The police told them to go back.

Go back! Go back! But they were
unafraid, because they were singing to God!
The police opened fire and now,
today after school.
I will go to bury my mother.

My father is like a tiger,
angry, pacing, ready to leap.
Among our people, he tells me,
the entire tribe must come
to send her to the other world.

The witch doctor must say the words
that will make her journey safe.
Now, that cannot be, because
we are on the house arrest.

What kind of people,
my father asks the darkness,
will not allow humans
to mourn their dead.

Thank God, he says to me, you are
not an infant. You are ten years old
and can look out for yourself, now.

But I must go away to fight!

We are on house arrest,
the government says
because violence *must* be
avoided.

I think of my mother, and suspect
that it is too late: violence has already happened.
And, I am afraid, that before too long
there will be much more.

Afrique Unique

In all of history, this heartless land
where children starve while diamonds
reflect bands
of platinum, of gold, of genocide
will tales of misery for centuries span

In all of history, this apartheid
which sounds to me, my friend
like apart- hate!
demands Mandelas sit in jail and rot
while all the world sits idly by and wait.

In all of history, have yet I heard
where man's not been allowed to
mourn his dead
where truth has in a heavy blanket hid
where God had seen yet not a word has said.

III

*

ETRE

---

*

etre -   Fr. - to be

be -   Blk. Amer. Eng. dialect - verb expressing state of being transcending all tenses and persons, thus regular.

We Be - Etre #1

I be
you be
he, she, it be
we be
you be
they be

how simple
how un - der - stand - able
but teacher say:
I can't be
I have to am
you have to are
and he is - and she.
we, like you, have to are
and they, of course,
being plural, are too.
but teacher don't
un - der - stand that
all the time,
all the time

me, my mama, pa
all of us
us,
we be.

We Be Family - Etre #3

Sometimes, on Saturdays, we be sitting around
the house, watching t.v.
we be eating popcorn and
talking during the commercials
we be laughing some
and having a good time.
                              We be family.

The House Where We Live - Etre #4

The house where we live
    don't be quiet all the time.
The people who live upstairs,
    be fighting most the time
The woman be saying:
    Ain't no money, ain't no food,
    Why you be drinking all the time
He say I don't know
    then beat her up, somemore
The children - they be crying
    and trying to help they mama
My mama say:
    I wish we could move from here.

Soft Be Heart – Etre #5

Soft be heart, so soft to touch
That it be sighing

Strong be love, so hard to beat
My ease to lying

Here to cry, love will not die
Though it cease weeping

Feel the slights - of lonely nights
               My heart be dying.

IV
OPPRESSION

my dreams

mama had dreams too, i know
but she was greatly over-powered
by the magnitude of pressures
from an unyielding society
that deemed she was a member
of a caste of lowly, unwinning
have-nots.

her dreams were destined
it was said, to fester
like a sore, and they did

yet i sprang from her, and
have dreams too
i will not be over-powered
by anything
as it also has been
written, I'll explode.

The Brightness of Fire

Fifty-six brutal blows, one balmy night
To its body and its head
made old Los Angeles sick.
For eighty one eternal seconds
its insides churned lava hot
then L.A. vomited
sick stuff all over itself.

Where vomit touched ground,
so hot it was,
a fire shot up until
thousands of frantic fires
roared and screamed in
brightness to the heavens.

The brightness of fire
blinded many who then
cried out, "Riot! riot!"
forgetting that a king
long dead once said,
"A riot is the language
of those without justice."

But because they could not see
could only smell the stink of smoke
could only feel the flesh-licking heat
could only sense the wrongness
of it all, they still cried riot.
.

For days, old Los Angeles
crawled in pain on its knees
regurgitating its rotten inners
like an old dog crawling
on all four, spewing maggots.

One balmy night,
because of fifty-six brutal blows
in eighty-one seconds
to its body and its head
old Los Angeles was very sick,
indeed.

Afterwards, others, glancing
distastefully at the hot vomit,
blamed the maggots and the fly.

The Cleansing

From college the words
have haunted me:
The catharsis of pity and fear,
a man causes doom,
the sages say
Through catharsis of pity and fear.

I think of the time
In a long ago place
When T. J. Turner died
We all was so scared
And sorry we were
The catharsis of pity and fear?

His wife, how she screamed
Poor Annie Lee Turner
With eight children clinging to her
When the Klan hung him up
And cut off his sex
And burned where it had been.

As they sped off in glee
In their beat-up old cars
Blowing dust in the faces of us
I wish then I'd known
That all that this was-was catharsis of pity and fear.

mama's hands

mama took in washing, yes
she did, had the cleanest
wash in town, washed by
hand, the sign said.
 peering through the window
 seeing hands abused by lye
 solution, burning water, steaming

mama hung the cleanest clothes
upon the line, in winter, she
was strong.
 peering through the frosted window
 fascinated by wet hands, that stuck
 to frozen other-people's clothes

mama had the nicest wash, folk
came down the unpaved road, from
way cross town, cause mama ironed.
 sitting in the big warm kitchen
 watching calluses when touching
 iron, make mama flinch

mama took them back unwrinkled
smelling clean, hand-delivered
sign said,
> *watching sadly as she started*
> *walking down the hardened road*
> *with labored burden to*
> *other side of town*

mama came home late at evening
rough hands brushing gently at
my tears, while asking, what's
the matter.
> *agonizing inwardly, knowing when*
> *i grew up, i would kill someone,*
> *anyone, for making mama's hands*
> *hurt*

Days of Splendor

I remember days of splendor
I recall the days of yore
I remember days of suffering
Blood did fall like rain does pour.

Days when masters ruled as gods.
Demanded life and brought forth death
Owned the very souls of men
Flesh and bones, the thought, the self.

Ruled the very means of thinking
With the tiny, snaky lash
Ruled, and asked complete submission
Ruled in days of splendor past.

I remember days of splendor
Lust unleashed on women Black
Children torn from sucking breast
Profits made on sweat-black backs.

Profits that brought pride, and glory,
Mansions and a life of splendor
Masters were the goodly buyers
Slaves, from pain, unwilling spender.

Days of splendor brought forth laughter
From the madmen, joy and glee
Brought forth sorrow to the sane
Horror from which some did flee.

Yet this madness is yet with us
Warping now, our daily life
For the memory of the madmen
Cleaves our pride, as though with knife.

Thoughts today of long-gone sorrow
Make us flush with shame, and cry
Why? Sane men in days of pity
Had to deal with grief. Or die.

In the days of splendor/horror
Men felt happiness and sorrow
Do we shame at thoughts of sorrow?
From madmen, their sickness borrow?

Let those who are guilty pity
Those who profited show shame
We who watch this crime, in silence
Must remember, though it pains.

I remember days of splendor
Days when men owned other men
Don't forget that mass men-madness
Lest the splendor starts again.

Communication Gap

Downtown, gentlemen confer, discussions take place.
Improved performance year, no significant net loss.

Discussions require hope, so folk here just rap
Naw, we ain't got no heat neither. Had the stove on
all night. Don't matter tho. Can't pay the bill, no how.
Despite uncertainties, good growth pattern anticipated.

Yeah, I heard Mis Mable's baby's back in County. Ate sa
moa dem paint chips.
*Improved performance year, economic climate reflects
outstanding performance.*

Landlord here today. Said don't worry 'bout the no hot
water. That's just cause the furnace's broke, that's all.
Revenues from operations represent substantial growth

I'm tired of dese peeling walls and no hot water and heat.
I'm getting plain mad,
*Efficient management of properties reflect in good growth
pattern.*

Where in the hell did I put that gun?
Despite uncertainties, revenues...

Hey man, I wanna talk to you.
If there's any difficulty, I'm sure we can discuss...

V

ALIENATION

.

Money in *Manteno

What's the use of money in Manteno
Can it replace the alter-ego lost
for the self that zombies in despair
Or calm the raging quiet desperation
compelling one forlorn... deranged
to savagely, till all is gone...
pull out one's hair?

What's the need of money in Manteno
Can money silence lonely voices crying
out in the nights to gods
that have no ears
Or resurrect an Id that sunk immobile
inactive from disquietude
and... nameless fears.

We sometimes go through life pursuing madness
As madmen masquerading pseudo madness
To reach the top and there to sit
... in decadence and opulence
Yet find ourselves like
slimy, tangled snakes
meandering in some deep somber pit.

*Manteno- Mental institution in Manteno, Illinois

Lonely In The Masses

Undoubtedly you think me mad
Because I am confined
Contrarily, you think you're sane
Because you're unrestrained.

You walk down lonely city streets
A stranger amongst the millions
Of other strangers' souls
And feel lonely in the masses.

You exist on hard, cold concrete blocks
Formed by geometric lines called streets
And robot like, "DO NOT WALK"
Or step on the lines. but at a given time
In unison.

You live in wee city boxes
That pimple the level earth
Boxes cluttered as close as possible
And stacked one upon the other.

You count the daily war toll
Into the hundreds of thousands
And precede the number
With "only".

You even sit in sacred houses
On days of "time-out"
After lying and cheating, yesterdays
And believe your soul is safe.

Yet I, wanting to be a part
Of this madness no longer
Attempted only to leap
From the openings of one of the boxes
                    Undoubtedly, you think me mad.

King

He rode down tired, used-up city streets
in splendor and in victory
The beer cans and broken glass did sparkle
in the sun like gems and precious shining diamonds
strown along his path.

The poor, life-beaten derelicts
his noble subjects cheered
To see him in his splendor;
pink suit and shoes, to match his hot-pink
custom Cadillac.

His harem, seated proudly to his right
and to the rear
Though ladies of the night were
presently dignitaries in majestic procession.
The little boys smiled, and the big ones
hoped to someday be the heir to just such
a total estate.
For riding down 47th Street that day was
his majesty: King Pimp.

Private Matters

I never liked the rain
too much
It had a sneaky, spiteful way
of getting me wet
whenever I was
in it.

And always the patterns
that most people
never saw.

Strange patterns of shapes unknown
So many colors
I never saw
before.

Strange! Yet most people
didn't seem to mind
the patterns
in rain.

But, of course
it didn't get
most people
wet.

VI
HOPE

Parenthood

Just as in obtaining life
there are two ways with a poem:

First, one can think a poem
Taking that which exists -
Claiming it for one's own
        Like adoption

Or, one can feel a poem
Having life within you -
Willing it to exit
        Like giving birth

Getting to The Promised Land

We tried so hard, Martin, for the plan
Of getting to the Promised Land.
You said with us you might not go
You wanted, though, for us to know
That *we* would reach the Promised Land
And then you left us, as He'd planned.
Well, Martin, that was long ago
Yet we can feel and sense and know
You taught us much while you were here
Where now we have a lingering fear
That like a bird with head in sand
We cannot see the Promised Land.

You showed us how to overcome
Showed without lifting hand or gun
How we could win a moral fight,
Reveal to all that we were right.
You gave to each of us a seat,
A vote, a job: in sweltering heat
A drink of water - fountain cold
You are somebody, we were told.
But that was, Martin, long ago
We all have sense enough to know
That something's wrong with this great plan
Of getting to the Promised Land.

It's not your fault, I truly add
But still the whole thing's too, too sad.
You gave us back our dignity
By challenging reality.
You ventured to the mountain top
Avalanche - like, nothing could stop
You but a bullet, in your heart,
Which was for you, your biggest part.
But Martin, that was oh so long
When words were sang to that sad song
Of We Shall Overcome, someday
When Promised Land was far away.

You told us that you had a dream
And we were glad: to us it seemed
That yes! there was a Godly plan
For getting to the Promised Land.
Yet there's no land within our sight
And some of us're too tired to fight
Again - Oh, Martin will there ever be
America that's truly free?

Some people wallow in despair
And act like they don't even care
About you or your famous plan
Of getting to the Promised Land.

Don't they remember - you went to jail
which for a Black man - was like Hell -

For them - don't they know that you bled -
For them - while in death's hands - you led
Us. To liberty - dignity
Dogs, hoses were reality
For them - God, please, say it's a lie:
That this great man did have to die
While still some live who cannot see
He died for you, he died for me,
And we can't implement his plan
For getting to the Promised Land?

O'mine eyes have seen the glory -
Was the last part of his story
Of the coming of the Lord! he
Had been to the mountain - could see
Over the top - Promised Land!!
He went on ahead, but the plan
Was that we, the people, would come,
All the world's just men - not some
Black men and white men, young and old
And what would this Promised Land behold:
Judgement by character - This Place
Not by the color of one's face.

He was the world's great gift from God
Allowed to come here - here to trod
Amongst us - to help - show the way
But we know he'd have to go someday.
He went from dirt roads to Nobel Prize
Showed us how a man could rise.
Yes, he was a King among kings.
In a world where his voice still rings.

To honor him, we must live right
Yet for our birthrights, always fight
And one day following his hand
We *will* get to the Promised Land.

PICKING BLACKBERRIES

I remember picking blackberries.
I see myself then: thin, scrawny
and "mama-greased-me" black
going down the dusty, foot-hot road
looking back at mama on the porch,
realizing now, the look she wore
was one of worry and uncertainty.

I'd morning at the patch
and pick and eat, pick and eat
until my silver buckets
could hold no more
Then I would eat and eat, eat and eat
Then start my journey home
my fingertips and lips
stained deeper black.

I remember moving from the South
and *my* uncertainty
"Are there blackberries up there?"
I asked mama on the train
"No, but more; no, but more"
her answer keeping beat with wheel's song.

I tried to tell my city friends
about picking blackberries, and the
deep-dish cobblers, mama used to make
but they looked at me all funny like
and they didn't understand, I know
Oh, so poor, Oh, so poor.

We prospered in the city, me and mama
she got a real good job with government
and I played basketball in the back alley
that earned a scholarship to U. of I.
Life was good, life was good,
Life was very good.

We went back home last year
to see the old folk
just me and mama, driving our new car
Our old shack gone, I went to visit
my childhood blackberry patch
and hopefully recapture memories
But in its place there stood a monstrous park
amusement park, complete with neon signs
    What a pity, what a pity.

VII
PAIN

STATEMENT ON CHILD ABUSE

If mothers cry when babies die
From aches too gross to bear
Or children cringe unconsciously
When threat of life comes near.

If fathers beat unmercifully
A child who cries from pain
Who later, screams, in silent dreams
From terror of the same.

If people burn the flesh of young
From sickness, or for pleasure
With butts of ashes hot
And feel no guilt or self-disgust
And seeks assistance not.

If we view via "tele-news"
These horrors that there be
And cry not out in protest
At the evils that we see
                    Can we condemn the rest?

A Night Of War

Splendored shades of darkness
prevailed with each fleeting moment
yet; *somewhere*
great bodies of men
were too occupied with
war and war machines,
to lift their eyes and admire the splendidness.

The last hint of lightness
fought desperately for existence
yet; *somewhere,*
equally great bodies of men
were too employed with guns and gunpowder
to raise their eyes and esteem the coming darkness.

Time passed. An eternity.
Dawn came, bringing with it
grandeur almost too great for the sky
to accommodate in its "one-ness".
Yet; still, men were too engaged with
killing and being killed,
to look to the heavens
and appreciate the beauty.

Must We Wait?

Must we wait, till it's too late
Before Man learns
Must we feel the air we breath
Pollute our lungs?

Must we see birds drop like rain
Before Man stops
Or feel earth whirl thru space
From heaviness
Much like a spinning top?

Must every nation build a bomb
Before we all feel safe
Must everyone ignite his bomb,
If one explodes, to just "save face"?

Must every fish drown in the muck
Before we see
That fish can't live in dirt and filth
Like we?

Must we wait, till it's too late
Before we know
We kill ourselves
As God reviews this foolish show?

If I Cry

If I cry when children die
Or feel my heart bewail
When I see children thin
And all they really constitute
Are skeletons with skin.

If I curse when I see worse
than death itself
When I see flesh dripping from
bones of a child afire
Who if she said she understood
What napalm was, would be a liar.

If I pain when I see men who's sane
Experiment on human being without
a shameful trace
And state they only hope or re-create
a super race.

If I hurt when I see dirt
Upon the streams
And fish that drown in liquid muck
that once was water
And land so barren that it's obscene
And surely would offend Our Father.

If I ache when atoms break
in chain reactions
And violate the very flesh of men
And then go on to mutate genes
And other sins.

If I cry when children die
And if my weeping does offend
Then say to me, "You only dream."
And I will cease.

If I Should Die Before I...

Today is April 6, 1944.
"Today," the teacher says, "we shall sing
Frere Jacques one more time."
What she means is – we shall sing
Frere Jacques one more time
before we die.
Our parents are already dead,
killed by the Nazi Gestapo of Lyon.

Now, we hear, the Nazis are coming here,
today, to this orphanage where we are
in the village of Izieu,
which is somewhere in France.

There are forty-four children here, all ages.
Some of us are French, but
some of us were born
in other countries.

The problem is that *all* of us are Jews
and the Nazis do *not* like Jews.
Therefore, we shall die soon.
So the teacher says, today,
"We shall sing Frere Jacques
one more time—Begin!"

And – Oh! – how we sing!
We sing with all our heart!
We sing with all our strength!

We sing with every atom of fleshly matter
in our mortal selves!

We sing so loudly, hoping God will hear us!
We sing beautifully, hoping He will look down
and say, "Do not harm those children
who sing so beautifully!
We sing with hope that God,
in hearing us, will thunder down
as he once did long ago,
"Let my people go!"

When we sing Frere Jacques,
we sing in rounds of pairs,
two children singing together.
Because there are forty-four children here,
we sing 22 rounds.
It takes a long time, but
we began singing in this matter
on long, cold winter nights
while we waited patiently to die.

So now, today, we are singing
Frere Jacques beautifully, loudly
with all our strengths, heart,
and hope, one more time.

Standing next to me is my friend, Etienne,
who is singing too fast.
He and I are supposed to be
singing together.
But I understand why
he is singing so fast.
He is afraid we will not finish
before we die.

I wonder does it hurt to die.
No, that is not what I mean,
It only takes moments to die,
therefore *that* pain is inconsequential.
What I mean is, does it hurt
to be dead.

But I cannot think of such things, now.
I must concentrate on
singing this song,
beautifully and perfectly.

Etienne is still singing
too fast. Should I catch up
with him and then sing faster,
so that we sing
in symphony?

Or should I continue to sing
at my pace, which is correct,
but forces us to sing
in disharmony?

It is a question whose answer
I do not know.
Nor is it an unimportant
question, I pose.
It is a worldly question.

Is it better to do a thing quickly,
but poorly, in order to complete it,
and have as a reward,
its completion,

or slowly, yet perfectly,
but chance not completing it
at all?

As we sing, Frere Jacques,
one more time,
I ponder over this question,
a troublesome one.

Through a long process
of thought and logic,
I finally arrive at an answer
to my question.

It is better, I feel,
to do a thing perfectly, because
there is a chance we will finish
and then—
it is done!

If we sing imperfectly
once we have finished,
we have an imperfect thing
completely done!

I take Etienne's hand in mine
shaking it in proper time
and singing loudly to beat,
forcing him to slow down.

He does and we continue
to sing. Oh! how we sing!
Then while singing
Frere Jacques, one more time
Etienne turns to me and
his eyes and his face
are smiling broadly.

He can see we will finish,
we *will* finish, we will finish
perfectly and we are so happy!

I look around the room and
I can see that all the children
are singing and happy and smiling.

I smile back.

I wonder why teacher wants us
to sing such a long, complicated song,
now.
But before I can think too hard
about this, I hear
in the distance,
the bleeping sirens
of the approaching Nazis.

But it does not matter now,
because we *will* finish—perfectly!!

*

On April 6, 1944, under the command of Klaus Barbie,
forty-four children and their five guardians were arrested at
the orphanage in the village of Izieu, deported, and murdered
in the gas chambers at Auschwitz. The characters and events
of this prose-poem, based on that historical phenomenon, are
fictitious. My sorrow that it occurred is real.

EPILOGUE

Freedom

Black bodies lying in the street!
Dying, yet still held down with boot-clad feet.
A trophy pose – the culmination of the kill
The killer's smile revealing a hunter's thrill.

Bang! Black bodies dying on city streets!
Lying face down – bullets in the back – beneath the silent sheets
Yellow tape swaying gently in the breeze
Innocent birds watching cautiously from urban trees.

Black bodies sighing on a city street!
Bleeding out on canvases of gray concrete
Red blood soaking in like graffiti artists coloring streets
Hands cuffed behind the back – cuffs on the feet.

Black bodies crying silently on city streets!
Dried tears frozen in time on young black cheeks
Not strange fruit, swinging from a Southern Poplar tree
But still as dead – in view for all to see.

A national shame, A new atrocity
Of killing us, hoodlessly, with sheer impunity.

LORETTA HAWKINS

PUBLISHED BY:

FIREKEEPER ARTISTRY
CHICAGO, ILLINOIS

ABOUT THE AUTHOR

LORETTA A. HAWKINS

(FIREKEEPER)

Loretta A. Hawkins is an American playwright, poet, author, social activist, spoken-word artist, and retired educator. Born in Winston-Salem, North Carolina, she grew up on the west side of Chicago, Illinois. She has earned five college degrees from Chicago City College, Illinois Teachers College, Governors State University and The University of Chicago. After having taught school for thirty-four years at every academic level, she reinvented herself as a spoken- word artist. She is the creator of four full-length plays, two educational workbooks, three children's books, a novel, a book of short fiction, and her poems have appeared in anthologies internationally. Hawkins' work, of various literary genres, have appeared in the following publications: *African Literature Today, Teaching Today, Major Poets, Individual Psychology Reporter, The University of Chicago Magazine, and Education Week*, among many others. She has won awards in all major genres. In 2016, she was awarded a Lifetime Achievement Award from the National Poetry Awards Society. Her first cd, *Only One Thing*, was awarded the Best Spoken-Word CD of 2017. Her play, *Of Quiet Birds* was recipient of First Place Prize for 2017 National *A Taste of Theater Playwriting Competition*. Her poetic name is Firekeeper, and she is a member of P.O.E.T. Inc. (People Of Extraordinary Talent.) For more information about her, Google: Loretta Hawkins /African Literature.

LORETTA HAWKINS

www.ingramcontent.com/pod-product-compliance
Lightning Source LLC
Chambersburg PA
CBHW032049040426
42449CB00007B/1036